The SIX TRUTHS OF

Motherhood

HOW *TO*
NAVIGATE CULTURE,

PARENT YOUR CHILDREN,

& STILL FIND TIME
FOR YOU

BY: KAREN STUBBS

Requests for information should be addressed to:
iDisciple, 13560 Morris Rd, suite 1140, Alpharetta, Georgia 30004.
ISBN: 978-0-9992813-5-2

TABLE *of* CONTENTS

A NOTE FROM KAREN

Welcome to the Six Truths of Motherhood study. This study is written for moms who find themselves feeling overwhelmed in their role, find it difficult to parent in a fast-paced culture, struggle with disciplining their children, feel bitter at times when life doesn't seem fair, and have lost their mojo as a woman. We have all been there. This study will give you the tools to navigate the difficult journey of motherhood and offer you some much-needed encouragement along the way. I hope and pray you will come away from this study feeling refueled and refreshed as a mom.

Karen

What you need to get the most out of this book:

Create a special place in your home. Find a favorite spot, a comfy chair, or a nook to go through the book.

Grab a cup of coffee, or a glass of tea and bring your Bible and a spirit ready to learn and grow.

ASK GOD TO OPEN UP YOUR HEART AND YOUR MIND TO HIS TRUTH.

OVERWHELMED

Session One

OVERWHELMED

Why do we get overwhelmed as moms? Well, probably because being a mom is overwhelming. The sheer fact that you are taking a newborn baby home from the hospital, without any training whatsoever, is overwhelming by itself. As the baby grows, so does the feeling of being overwhelmed. Think about it! You go from one stage of life to another, experiencing it all for the first time and not knowing what you are doing. It is as if you are taking a trip to London and the Captain came to your seat and said, "I need you to fly the plane. I've got a manual you can follow, but it's all up to you." If you are like me, you would be feeling a little overwhelmed. For most moms, that is what it is like in being a parent. The emotions we feel, dealing with the "unknown," and of course, guiding another human being — it is all overwhelming.

Just being around other moms often gave me a sense of being overwhelmed. When I was around other moms with their children, I would "see" all they were doing as moms, and it made me second guess my decisions as a mom.

Having more than one child is overwhelming because you think that baby #2 will be exactly like baby #1, but no! Each of my four children were very different in every way, which made my job harder as a mom. Not only did I not know how to discipline, love, and pour into one child, I had four children who all needed different things from me.

Our lives are busy before having kids, but once children arrive, the demands on your schedule increase immensely, especially as they get older. Children's schedules are also very demanding, mainly when you are responsible for driving them from place to place. The other things that increase are the laundry, the cleaning, and the constant chore of cooking. Let's also not forget the weight all moms carry of meeting the needs of the family. You know the drill. "Mom, I need you." "Mom, can you help me?" "Mom, come with me." "Mom, why?" I used to get so tired of my children calling out to me, "Mom." I remember one day I told Greg, "If I hear 'mom' one more time, I might blow a gasket." Do you ever feel this way?

Don't forget one of our most important jobs as a mom is to discipline our children. Good grief! That is bound to send any mom into a frenzy of overwhelmed emotions! The constant worrying: "Am I doing this right?" "Is it working?" "Am I too permissive?" "Am I too strict?" All of these thoughts and emotions are hard on us moms.

This study is designed to take an honest look at the life of a mom and her journey. In order to get the most out of the curriculum, it is important that you, as a mom, are willing to be honest about your struggles and weaknesses. No mom has it all together, and we all need our Heavenly Father. Jesus said it best in 2 Corinthians 12:9, "My grace is sufficient for you, for my power is made perfect in weakness."

Learn to lean into Jesus in your weakness and to receive His power in your journey of motherhood. In the following pages, journal your thoughts and be transparent with yourself and God.

There are three key emotions that we can feel as a mom:

1. *Inadequacy*

Inadequate means insufficient, and insufficient means lacking competence.

If we are all really honest with ourselves, a lot of the time we feel insufficient when parenting our children. When your child gets hurt, whether on the playground or when a friend is mean to them and hurts their heart, our words as a mom are insufficient. We realize that this pain our child is experiencing is part of life, and no matter how hard we try, we cannot take it away. That fact leaves us feeling inadequate. Even when your child gets physically ill, you can take them to the doctor for medicine, but sometimes they just have to wait it out. In those times, we also feel inadequate. What about the "real life" issues your children may have? Maybe they struggle with a learning disability, or a weight problem, or severe acne—as a mom, you cannot fix these things for them. That's when we feel inadequate.

Journal

Take a moment and write out areas you feel inadequate as a mom.

....

....

....

....

....

2. Uncertainty

To be uncertain is to be doubtful.

Until we have some experience under our belts, moms, most of the time, we doubt our decisions. These doubts start with our newborns and progress with each stage of life.

Newborn
Should I let them cry or go get them?
Should I start food when the doctor says it is okay, or do I wait?
Should I leave them in the nursery at church or keep them with me?
Should I put them on a schedule, or do I let the child determine the schedule?

Toddler
How do I discipline?
What is an action that requires discipline, and what is just normal for this stage of life?
How do I get my toddler to stop whining?
How do I get my toddler to sleep through the night?
Do I put them in preschool? How many days?

Elementary Age
What type of school do I put them in? Home school? Private? Public?
How do I control the friends my child has?
What is acceptable discipline for this age?
How do I instill confidence in my child?
How do I teach my child to stand up for themselves?
How do I shepherd my child's heart?

Middle School
What is normal behavior?
Why is my child pulling away from me? How can I stop that?
How can I help my child be secure in themselves and not follow the crowd?
When do I step in, and when do I step back?

High School
How do I step into a coaching role with my teen?
How do I give my child independence and responsibility?
Do I stay on my child about their grades? College?
How do I build my teenager up and create a good relationship with them?
How do I set my teen up for success?
How do I get my teen to see their actions have consequences?

No wonder us moms doubt ourselves 24/7. There is a lot going on in our minds. Once again, if you have more than one child, this list is multiplied by the number of children you have.

KEY VERSE: ISAIAH 40:31 (NKJV)

*But those who **wait** on the Lord*
Shall renew their strength;
They shall mount up with wings like eagles,
They shall run and not be weary,
They shall walk and not faint.

Journal

In what areas are you feeling uncertain as you parent?

....

....

....

....

....

....

....

....

....

3. *Insecurity*

Insecure means not to be confident, or sure of yourself.

Since the life of a mom is so uncertain, it naturally breeds insecurity. How can a mom be secure in her actions, thoughts, and plans if most of the time she is guessing how to manage her children? Moms also are insecure when they "try" something new, possibly a new way to discipline, but it doesn't seem to work. At best, it can feel like you are hitting your target about half the time in parenting.

Journal

Write out your thoughts and feelings and insecurities you've faced in motherhood.

....

....

....

....

....

....

....

....

....

There are also two truths that add to our sense of being overwhelmed, and those are:

- *Parenthood is a marathon.*
- *There are no shortcuts in parenting.*

Many times, we enter parenthood with the mindset of *"How hard can this be?"* After a few months or years, we realize it is just beginning. Parenting is a marathon, and we need to set our minds up for a long race. Marathon runners do not just go out and run 26.1 miles in a day. No, they train for it, they map out a plan, and stick to the plan. Greg has run several marathons, and I know that it takes lots of training and work. It's the same with parenting. It is not a short sprint; it is a race that requires discipline, endurance, and strength.

In this marathon, there is another key component. There are no shortcuts. If you, as a runner, want to run a good race, and finish the marathon with a decent time, then you cannot take shortcuts. In the months prior to the race, you must put in the work. Each day, you will need to be running, different lengths of runs, different styles of running, and every so often, you will need to do a long endurance run to prepare for the marathon. Moms, it is the same way in parenting. There are no shortcuts in discipline, shepherding your child's heart, or teaching your child right from wrong. There are no quick fixes. So many moms get overwhelmed in this LONG process of parenting, and they wonder when their child will "get it." It takes time and maturity. Don't give up!

Those who hope in the Lord will Renew their Strength

This is the reality for all of us moms: Our FEELINGS begin to dictate how we view ourselves and how we view ourselves dictates how we believe God views us. When we do that, we tell ourselves:

> God is disappointed in us.
>
> I'm the wrong mom for this child.
>
> I should do more.
>
> I'm not enough.
>
> It's on me to fix the situation.

Before you know it, we begin to parent through our emotions which only adds to our feeling of being overwhelmed. We end up NOT taking our burdens to God because we want to get our act together before we go to God for help.

Now that we have established why being a mom is so overwhelming, what is a mom to do?

KEEP IN MIND,
GOD KNOWS OUR CIRCUMSTANCES, AND HE KNOWS
WE ARE OVERWHELMED.

ISAIAH 40:11
He tends his flock like a shepherd:
He gathers the lambs in his arms and carries
them close to his heart;
He gently leads those that have young.

He doesn't just leave us there either. He gives us a solution. The solution is found in Isaiah 40:31.

ISAIAH 40:31 (NKJV)
*But those who **wait** on the Lord*
Shall renew their strength;
They shall mount up with wings like eagles,
they shall run and not be weary,
they shall walk and not faint.

A key word in the verse is WAIT. In Hebrew, the word wait is "Qavah," which translated means "bind together." Think of a rope, how it has many strands that are bound together; in their binding, the rope gets its strength.

As a mom, do you want new strength? You must bind yourself together with God and His word to find new strength. How do we bind ourselves to God?

One way to bind yourself to God is to memorize Scripture. In binding yourself to God's Word, you are replacing your weakness for His strength. You are exchanging your lies for His truth. The lies that you are inadequate, uncertain, insecure. You can replace those lies with the truth that He is beyond adequate and certain of all things, and you are secure in His kingdom, His ultimate plan for your life, and the lives of your children. Three key areas you may need help with in binding yourself to God's Word are: Patience, Being Loving, Persevering.

Key Verses for New Strength in Patience

PSALM 37:7
Be still before the Lord and wait patiently for him;
do not fret when people succeed in their ways,
when they carry out their wicked schemes.

PSALM 40:1
I waited patiently for the Lord;
he turned to me and heard my cry.

PROVERBS 14:29
Whoever is patient has great understanding,
but one who is quick-tempered displays folly.

PROVERBS 15:18
A hot-tempered person stirs up conflict,
but the one who is patient calms a quarrel.

Key Verses for New Strength in Loving

I CORINTHIANS 13:4-7
Love is patient, love is kind. It does not envy, it does not boast, it is not proud. It does not dishonor others, it is not self-seeking, it is not easily angered, it keeps no record of wrongs. Love does not delight in evil but rejoices with the truth. It always protects, always trusts, always hopes, always perseveres.

Key Verses for New Strength in Persevering

HEBREWS 12:1
Therefore, since we are surrounded by such a great cloud of witnesses, let us throw off everything that hinders and the sin that so easily entangles. And let us run with perseverance the race marked out for us.

RESPOND

When we are overwhelmed as moms, God wants us to learn to bind ourselves to Him. Imagine a rope with all the threads bound together. Now list some ways you can bind yourself to God.

REFLECT

We all bind ourselves to something.

Some examples are:
- *Friends*
- *Spouse*
- *Financial security*
- *Social media*

What are you binding yourself to?

....

....

....

....

....

....

....

....

....

....

....

We are going to bind ourselves to something. We have the choice of whether we will be binding ourselves to our feelings or God's truth. When I bind myself to my emotions, it drains me. When I bind myself with God, He gives me NEW STRENGTH.

> Not recycled,
> Not borrowed,
> Not fake,
> I have NEW STRENGTH!

YOU WILL WALK AND NOT GET WEARY.
ISAIAH 40:31

People ask me, "How did you do it?" My answer has always been... by relying on God *Not family, not other support, just God*. I literally leaned into God for my help. I am not superwoman, but I did rely on God.

FINAL THOUGHT

As moms, we do not have to be overwhelmed, regardless of our circumstances. You can tap into the strength that exists outside your emotions and circumstances, and God stands ready to give it to you. It's your choice.

Peace comes from God's strength.

Moms, you and I have the profound privilege of creating a new climate in our homes. And the degree to which we lean into this principle and into God's strength will determine the atmosphere we want to create in our home.

You set the tone for your house.

Write out which atmosphere you want within your home: Overwhelmed or peaceful?

Journal

....

....

....

....

....

....

....

....

A NOTE FROM KAREN

What we want for you at Birds On A Wire is to experience the peace God offers to us.

What are you binding yourself to?

- *Friends*
- *Husband*
- *Wine*
- *Social media*

Think about how you could be binding yourself to God.

- *New music playlist*
- *Daily devotional*
- *Healthier habits (and one less glass of wine!)*
- *Scripture*
- *Finding a mentor*

Whatever it takes to bind yourself to God, do it!

If you will do that this week, not only will you feel less overwhelmed, but you will create a climate in your home that is not based on how you feel, but how He sees you and the family He gave you.

QAV

A H

Definition: to bind together

Session Two

HOLD THE LINE PT.1

F amily is a word that is near and dear to my heart. People ask me what I'm passionate about. My answer is: my family and Mexican food. My whole world is built around my family. I save my money all year for a family vacation. I sacrifice for my family. I'm willing to take one for the team for my family. Family trumps all things in my book. Whether you came from a great family or not, I believe most moms want a great family. Why wouldn't you? You are already investing your time, energy, and money into your family, so why not make it the best it can be?

I don't know about you, but I feel like our families are under attack these days. I am seeing more and more moms getting discouraged and ready to give up the fight.

What do I mean by under attack? Well, it feels harder and harder to parent these days! When I feel like I'm parenting in a wise way, I get so much push back.

- *When Kelsey and Abby were little, they had kidney reflux and had to take an antibiotic every day for maintenance. You have no idea how much push back I got about that from other moms. I felt under attack.*

- *I often felt under attack just trying to discipline my children. I'm not talking about spanking, just the simple act of saying "no" to my child. Other parents made me feel like an ogre, even when my child clearly needed to be told "no."*

- *Sometimes I felt under attack because I placed boundaries around myself and didn't allow my children to walk all over me.*

• *I've even felt under attack because I don't allow my daughter to wear shorts that I feel show too much. I'm labeled old-fashioned or a stick in the mud.*

• *You may even feel under attack if you don't want your kindergartner going to school with an iPad or iphone.*

Do you get what I'm saying? It's getting harder and harder to parent. We begin to feel like freaks for sticking to our principles!

Faced with this criticism and differences in opinion from other parents, how do you hold the line within your family? What does "hold the line" even mean?

"HOLD THE LINE" MEANS TO MAINTAIN AND PRESERVE A POSITION AGAINST ATTACK, OPPOSITION, OR CHANGE.

Holding the line takes guts, strength, and determination

I think you could argue that our families in 2018 are under attack, and there is a lot of change going on all around us. So, how do we hold the line? The term hold the line actually comes from football. Think of a football team lining up on the field. The ball is hiked and the defense is holding the line, trying not to let the offense break through. Well, that's our job as moms. We need to hold the line and not allow the enemy to break through. Can it be done? Yes, but it takes guts, strength, and determination.

There are four areas where I believe that we, as moms, can hold the line.

1. *BE the parent.*
2. *Aim for ideal.*
3. *Protect family time.*
4. *Foster financial freedom.*

1 BE THE PARENT.

Let's get started with the first area: BE the Parent. What does that mean?

This is a lot harder than it sounds. First off, it's our first time around as a parent, so therefore half the time we don't know what we are doing. It's like I told Greg when Kelsey was two, "I am arguing with a two-year-old, and she's winning!" Funny, but true. To "BE the Parent" means I, as a parent, know what I'm doing, right? So, when I tell my child it's time for bed and they push back and say, "I'm not sleepy," do I listen to them? Do I say, "Okay, I get that because I don't want to go to bed when I'm not sleepy either." Or do I say, "Sorry! You are five years old, and you don't get to decide when you want to go to bed. I'm your parent."

Children can make you second guess your decisions, but at the end of the day, one thing you will always have on your children is age and life experience. Don't discount that one thing. There is a natural hierarchy in parenting: you are the parent, the authority, the one that has to make the hard calls at times. Sometimes, it means you're not the one that not everyone likes, but it's your job.

EPHESIANS 6:1-3
Children, obey your parents in the Lord, for this is right.
"Honor your father and mother"
—which is the first commandment with a promise—
"so that it may go well with you and that
you may enjoy long life on the earth."

What BE the Parent is NOT:

A friend
- **You are not your children's friend.**
- Your child has lots of friends, but only one mom.
- Love your child the right way: a godly and wise way.

Your child has lots of friends, but only one mom.

Your child has lots of friends, but only one mom and that is you. You need to be the wise person in your child's life, the one who tells them truth instead of what they want to hear. Friends tell each other what they want to hear, but a parent should be the experienced and authoritative voice, giving wise counsel.

A shield
Don't shield your child from consequences; you aren't shielding, just delaying the consequences.

If you take on the job of being your child's shield, always protecting them from getting hurt feelings, or making sure your child is always being treated fairly, then you are just delaying the "hurt" for your child. When your child hits adulthood, there will not be anyone protecting them from the hurts of life. "BE the Parent" means guiding your child through the hurt, and teaching them how to move past the hurt, and helping them to deal with it. It is easier to learn those lessons when you are young than as an adult.

Tips on Being the Parent

You have three voices as a mom:
- Teacher voice: Helping your child learn what they don't know.
- Coach voice: Guiding your child along the way.
- Counselor voice: Seeking to understand what your child is feeling.

BIRTH TO 5 YEARS OLD
Laying the Foundation: Teacher Voice

Teach your child about authority and submission.
- This is a Biblical concept, God set up authority from the beginning of time.
- Help your child understand the hierarchy.
- How will your child learn right from wrong, morals, and values? Teach your child to treat others the way we want to be treated.

Don't apologize for being the authority in your child's life. You don't need to hold it over your children, but do let them know from toddler years that you are the boss. Submission to authority will be a concept your child will have to deal with for the rest of their lives, so it is better to teach them while they are young. Adults submit to authority all the time, whether with law enforcement, paying taxes, or with a boss. Submission is part of life.

Don't apologize for being the authority in your child's life.

6-12 YEARS OLD
Teacher voice/Counselor voice

Teacher: Give your child the reason behind your no's.
- Why we don't cheat
- Why we don't lie
- Why we don't steal
- Why we obey authority
- Why your character means everything

During these years, you combine your teacher voice with the counselor voice. A counselor seeks to understand. During these years, ask your child questions to help you understand their actions.

Counselor: Seek to understand, ask questions.
- Why did you do that?
- What was your thought process?
- How did that make you feel?
- Would you do anything differently?

These questions help a parent to understand where a child is coming from, and in turn, help us know how to guide them.

13-18 YEARS OLD

Counselor/Coaching Voice

While a coach is direct, the counselor seeks to understand.

- Teach your child to take responsibility for their actions.
- Teach your child that their actions have consequences.

During these years, you fluctuate between a coaching and counseling voice.

The Coach voice is direct.
A coach is always wanting the best out of his players, and a good coach will teach the team not just about the strategy of the game, but also lessons in life. The same is true with parenting. During the teen years, we, as parents, have so many opportunities to coach our children about life.

Counselor seeks to understand.
A counselor guides and directs, but lets the child figure things out for themselves. If a child figures out the problem for themselves, they are more likely to remember it for a lifetime. In parenting during these teen years, resist the urge to always "fix" things for your child. Let them struggle to figure it out. We all learn in the struggling.

Does a parent need to be more of a coach or a counselor during the teen years? You need to be both with your teens.

Be THE
Parent.

- EPHESIANS 6:1-3 -

2 AIM FOR THE IDEAL PRINCIPLES.

In a world where nothing seems to be sacred anymore, why not fight for the ideal? You may not achieve it, but you surely will never achieve it if you never try to put it as a goal. Sometimes I think, as moms, it's not that we don't want to have high ideals, it's that we feel so overwhelmed. We feel like we are fighting a losing battle. We get this way with other things, too. We take on the attitude of, "What's the point?" and we give up. Our weight is a clear example. We say, "I will never look like I did when I was 20." Then, we eat donuts, chips, forget to exercise, and gain five pounds. Another area we do this is with money. We will get tired of staying on budget, tired of driving the same old car, tired of wearing the same pair of shoes and clothes, and go out and splurge because we feel like, "What the heck? I'm tired of this." When we feel defeated in an area of our lives, ANY area, we give up.

For moms, parenting is no different. Why should I be the only crazy mom among my friends that expects such a high standard from my child, when more than likely, my child will be sassy and disrespectful to me? More than likely my child will fight with their siblings, more than likely my child will have sex before they are married, more than likely my son will look at porn, more than likely my child will experiment with drinking before 21 and occasionally do drugs. But, moms, this is not five pounds we are talking about; it's not a new car or pair of shoes.

IT IS YOUR CHILD'S LIFE. YOUR CHILD WILL FOR SURE NEVER ATTAIN IDEAL PRINCIPLES IF YOU NEVER TALK ABOUT THEM, TEACH THEM, AND ENCOURAGE THEM TO STAY STRONG.

Do you know how many conversations I had with ALL of my children over the years concerning these areas? Lots! I sat across from my girls and told them the importance of waiting until marriage to have an intimate relationship, why they should respect me and their dad, to treat their siblings with love and not hate, why Greg and I didn't allow boy/girl sleepovers, and how pornography affects you in your marriage. It wasn't one conversation: it was many, over many years. Remember, we are teachers first.

Finally, brothers and sisters, whatever is true, whatever is noble, whatever is right, whatever is pure, whatever is lovely, whatever is admirable -if anything is excellent or praiseworthy- think about such things.

PHILIPPIANS 4:8

Tips on Holding to Ideal Principles

Explain the why behind the no.
Don't just say no. Tell your children why.

- Why they aren't allowed to talk back to you.
- Why we, as a family, support each other and choose to talk lovingly to each other.
- Why you don't need an iPhone in kindergarten.
- Why we put parental blocks on the computers in the house.
- Why God says sex is awesome, but it is best when saved for marriage.
- Why we aren't allowing any drinking until the age of 21.
- Why recreational drugs are not okay, even under supervision.

They will not always understand why some of the things they want to do are not age appropriate; sometimes the answer is no and they must trust the no. Sometimes your children just need to trust you and know that you have their best interest at heart.

A few tools to use when teaching the Ideal Principles:

- *Empathy* is a very powerful tool with your children. You can have empathy for all those areas listed above. Key phrases: I understand. I know it's hard. I understand what you are going through.
- *Be present.* Close your computer, and put the phone down to talk with your child. Remember teaching your child to treat others the way you want to be treated? Don't we all want our husbands to listen when we are talking to them? It's the same with our children.
- *Create a safe environment* for your child to talk to you. Even when your child messes up—because they will. It's okay, perfection is not our goal.

Empathy is a very powerful tool with your children.

Creating a safe environment for your child can make you feel uneasy and uncomfortable at times as mom because you might find yourself talking about topics that you are not ready to discuss. Keep in mind, though, that your child is willing to talk to you and trust you, so you need to step up and talk, even though you may be uncomfortable. For instance, when Taylor was in high school, I was cleaning up the kitchen one night, and he came into the kitchen.

He said, "Mom, I want to talk to you about something." (That is usually code for "this might be uncomfortable.") I said to Taylor, "Of course, what's on your mind?" Taylor then started asking me questions about "why" pornography was bad and why everyone did it. Side note, as a mom, I was NOT ready for this conversation. I instantly started praying in my brain, asking God to give me wisdom. Taylor asked me what the big deal was. Since God will forgive all your sins and gives His grace too, why does it matter?

Whew! I felt trapped. Taylor was right: God does forgive, and He does give grace. However, I knew from my time working at a church in the counseling world the consequences of pornography in marriage and the damage it did. Once again, I started praying. There was a cookie cake on the counter, and I had an idea. I said to Taylor, "You are right, God does forgive and He for sure gives grace. Let's say your future marriage is this cookie cake. God's plan for you from the beginning of time is that you enter marriage pure and are faithful to your spouse your entire marriage. Yet every time you look at pornography, you are taking something away from your marriage." I grabbed a glass and started punching out holes in the cake. I punched out about six holes. I then told Taylor, "You are right, though, God forgives and gives us all grace, even when we mess up. So, God comes behind you and forgives you, and restores your life, like only God can do." Then I started putting the holes back in the cookie cake. I said to Taylor, "Now, you meet your future wife one day, and you are so excited about her and marriage, but what does your cake look like?" Taylor said, "It doesn't look good." I said, "It is whole, and has been put back together by God, but there are consequences from your choices."

Taylor stood there, thought for a minute, and said, "I've never thought about that before, Mom. Thank you for telling me."

Taylor and I had other conversations about pornography over the years; I wish I could say we only had one. I do know that because he felt "safe" with me, as his mom, we were able to talk through a touchy subject. Safe environments are key to building strong relationships with your children in the tough teen years.

It is never too late to start doing the right thing; teaching how to restart is an important skill. We all need to learn to "fail forward," learning from our mistakes.

A restart helps "reset" strong principles.
Teach your child how to restart when discipline is required. For example, if your daughter has stayed out too late on a date, the next date might mean watching a moving in the basement with little sister. Some restarts need coaching. You'll have to bring in the voices of the authority, counselor, teacher, and coach.

Don't feel guilty. You are the parent, so discipline is necessary because you love your children.

Examples of how to restart:
Let's start from the younger ages and work our way up.

TODDLER
- Clean up the mess after playing with toys.
- Temper tantrums mean doing extra chores around the house.
- Fussing with siblings means saying you are sorry with a hug and telling them you love them.

ELEMENTARY AGE
- Cheating in school: Walk them through why it is wrong and have them apologize to the teacher.
- Not being a good friend: Teach them what being a good friend means, and ask how it feels when others are not nice to them.
- Being a good sport: Winning is not everything. Teach your child how to be a good sport, even when they lose.

MIDDLE SCHOOL
- Cell phone: Abusing the privilege means losing the privilege.
- Showing disrespect to teachers requires an apology.
- Grades: If your child brings home a failing grade, teach them how to raise their grade (i.e, go in early to ask for help or extra work).
- Gossiping: explain the damage and hurt that it causes.

HIGH SCHOOL
- Minor driving mishaps: Make them pay for repairs or tickets.
- Drinking/Drugs: Making responsible choices brings extra privileges.
- Going too far in a physical relationship or having sex: Just because you messed up once, doesn't mean you should keep doing it. We all make mistakes. Learn and move on.

The bottom line for you, the mom, is to LOVE your child through anything and everything. Don't be naive and think your child will "never" stray. ALL children have a sinful nature. ALL children will slip up. It's your job to love them through it when they do.

RESPOND

Why is it hard to hold the line with your child? Are you afraid they won't like you? Are you afraid you will push them away? Will you commit today to be brave and begin to hold the line with your children?

List the ways you will accomplish this desire.

List the ways you can be the parent with your child.

1. ....

2. ....

3. ....

What are your ideal principles you want for your family?

....

....

List some ways you can achieve these goals with your family.

....

....

....

....

....

....

....

....

FINAL THOUGHT

You would never drop your child off in the middle of the Atlantic Ocean and tell them to swim to Florida, so don't let them grow up without your guidance as a parent. They need you to hold the line and keep them from getting in over their heads.

Journal

....

....

....

....

....

....

....

....

....

....

....

....

....

A NOTE FROM KAREN

Moms,
I know it is hard to hold the line with your children, but it is
worth it in the long run. Do the hard work now and reap the
benefits later. Your children are worth the extra effort.

YOUR CHILD
FRIENDS
ONE

HAS LOTS OF
BUT ONLY
MOM.

Session Three
HOLD THE LINE PT.2

I n this session, we are going to look at two more areas where we, as moms, should be holding the line.

- Protecting family time
- Fostering financial freedom

What does it mean to "hold the line?"

Hold the line means to maintain and preserve a position against attack, opposition, or change.

Key Scripture:

DEUTERONOMY 6:6–7
*And these words that I command you today shall be on your heart.
You shall teach them diligently to your children, and shall talk
of them when you sit in your house, and when you walk by the way,
and you lie down, and when you rise.*

Family Time
What is family time? It's a time during the evening (or on the weekend) when families are together talking, working on homework, relaxing, or being entertained. It's time that they enjoy together.

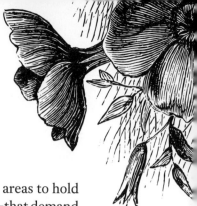

I don't know about you, but family time is almost the hardest of all areas to hold the line. There are so many activities—social, clubs, work, errands—that demand our time. How in the world do I hold the line on family time? This past summer, Taylor was working and Abby was babysitting, then going off with her friends all the time. Honestly, it was just easier to let everyone go their own way. But, we are still a family under one roof, and we still should be connecting with each other. Family time is crucial. Moms ask me all the time how to create a close-knit family. The answer is simple: Carve out family time. Fight for it!

Think of family time like the childhood game Tag. Remember home base, where you were safe to catch your breath, get a new game plan, then head out again for the chase? Everyone needed time on home base to re-group. It's the same with our family. Family time is where you catch your breath and gather a new game plan for life. It's where you are safe. Family time is where you are loved, accepted, and challenged. It's where you become a better person.

What is home base? It's where you:
CATCH YOUR BREATH
GET A GAME PLAN
FEEL SAFE FROM THE OUTSIDE WORLD

This generation needs a place to catch their breath from the fast pace of life, whether in middle school, high school, or college. The pace and the pressures are frantic. They need a place where no one can attack them, and they feel secure. Your family should offer a safe haven.

Home base offers a place to get a game plan for studying, exercising, dating, and simply relaxing. Your family is where your child knows they are loved and accepted, and it doesn't matter how many "likes" they have on their latest social media post.

Tips for Creating Family Time

- Eat dinner around the table more often than not.
- Designate family night (Examples: watch a movie, play a game, go out to eat, go bowling, hike up a mountain, camping, etc.).
- Create a safe environment:
    - a loving, accepting place
    - a fun place where they want to be
    - pay attention to different wirings/personalities
- Give your kids some ownership in family time. Let them decide what to talk about or where to go.
- Create an environment where your children feel safe to talk to you. Remember the Counselor Voice: You seek to understand. If your child opens up, don't judge or scold, just listen.

Tips on Protecting Family Time

- Prioritize
    - In a world where everyone and everything is wanting "more" from you, make your family your #1 priority.
- Model
    - As the parent, model the way for your children. You may need to reprioritize a few things in your life to get your family back in the #1 position.
- Start the family time habit when your children are young.
- Create family time outings while the children are small, and they will look forward to these outings as they grow older. Start mini-traditions that they can look forward to, like Sunday night spaghetti dinners or Saturday afternoon matinees.
- Get creative!
- Even in the busiest seasons, carve out time for family. Tailgate at the ball field or enjoy a family brunch at a local restaurant.

Foster Financial Freedom

If family time is the hardest area to hold the line, then finances are the least fun. I'm a fun kind of girl, and I like my stuff. It's true! So, the fact that I'm including finances in this talk tells you how important I think it is. Why? Well, in a world that thrives on materialism, it honestly goes back to the simple fact that if you don't hold the line on Finances, you are truly teaching your child an unrealistic view of money and a very narcissistic way of thinking. Living within your means requires a reality check every day, but it is a healthy way to live. It's not always a fun way to live, but it forces you to stay grounded. The hard part of this one is we live in a very affluent area, and we look around and think, "Why can't I have that?" We all must be realistic about what we can afford and what we cannot.

Basic Principle:

MATTHEW 6:21

For where your treasure is, there your heart will be also.

Verses:

1 CHRONICLES 29:11-13

Yours, O Lord, is the greatness, the power, the glory, the victory,
and the majesty. Everything in the heavens and on earth is yours,
O Lord, and this is your kingdom.
We adore you as the one who is over all things.
Wealth and honor come from you alone, for you rule over everything.
Power and might are in your hand, and at your discretion
people are made great and given strength.
O our God, we thank you and praise your glorious name!

1. TEACH RESPONSIBILITY

Take care of your belongings and be willing to share with others.

How to be responsible
- Preschool: Share with your friends.
- Elementary: If you break a toy, then replace it;
  buy a new one with your own money.
- High School: Take responsibility for your "things" and treat them well.

2. TEACH STEWARDSHIP

Give, save, spend.
Teach your children the principle of giving 10%, saving 10%, and spending the rest. The amount starts off small, but as they grow, it will grow with them.

3. TEACH OWNERSHIP

Three Principles of Ownership
- Take pride in your belongings.
- Contribute to their purchase or care.
- You break, you replace.

Example: Your child must save $1,000 towards having the privilege to drive a car in the family. This gives your child some ownership, and they will, in turn, take better care of the car. When our children were teenagers, we made them start buying birthday gifts for their friends and pay for social outings. For prom dresses, I set the price I was willing to pay, and if my daughters wanted a nicer dress, they had to contribute.

- Teach responsibility and generosity.
- You can never out give God!
- Teach your child about money and how to save, spend, and give. It all belongs to God, and we are supposed to leverage it for His kingdom. Let them experience this truth from an early age.
- There is a sense of deep accomplishment when you save money, and you feel good about yourself.
- Live by example. Let them see how you handle your finances and how you make decisions.
- When you say "no" to their request, explain the concept of need vs want.
- Expose your children to true need and how to have compassion. International mission trips are a great way to teach this principle.

THE GOAL IS FOR CHILDREN TO REALIZE THE VALUE OF MONEY, BUT ALSO TO UNDERSTAND THAT MONEY DOESN'T MAKE YOU HAPPY.

When you are working to hold the line, you will always be fighting against things, but you must stay focused on what you are fighting FOR.

	Against	*For*
BE THE PARENT	*What's popular*	*What's best/wise*
IDEAL PRINCIPLES	*Instant gratification*	*Future hopes/dreams*
FAMILY TIME	*Being an island*	*Team*
FINANCES	*Materialism*	*True satisfaction*

HOME
SHOULD BE A
SAFE PLACE.

RESPOND

Empathy is a powerful tool to use with your children. A parent can be empathetic and still hold the line. Write a few scenarios you can empathize with your child.

List ways to create a safe home.

1. ....

2. ....

3. ....

Teaching your child to be responsible takes time. List ways you plan on accomplishing this goal.

....

....

....

....

....

....

....

....

....

....

FINAL THOUGHT

Moms, if you aren't willing to hold the line, who will?

Are you willing to stand firm in a culture that is anything but firm, and be courageous to live a life set apart? Live a fulfilling life, a life with no regrets. You'll be rewarded with children who want to come home, because it is there that they find a safe haven from the rest of the world.

It's worth it. My prayer is that everyone will start living that kind of life, not a life of defeat or asking. "What's the use?" But a life where God conquers all.

To hold the line means to not allow the enemy to gain any ground. In order to do that, we, as moms, need to be aware when the enemy is moving in. Be on the lookout and ask God to give you wisdom. Pray and ask God to guide you and keep you strong.

Journal

....

....

....

....

....

....

....

....

....

A NOTE FROM KAREN

Raising children is not for the faint of heart. I know it is hard, but I also know you can do it! Don't give into what society says. Stick with your gut, even when you feel you are the only parent doing so. Your children will thank you in the end.

"I am not a pe
I am perfectly
for m

ect parent, but aired by God hild."

KAREN STUBBS

Session Four
DISCIPLINE

Everybody always wants to talk about discipline and what works *(or doesn't work)* for them. Discipline is difficult, to put it mildly. If you could take the need to discipline out of being a parent, then our job would be so much easier. Discipline is a hot topic, but it is also fully loaded! Before we begin, let's acknowledge a few things:

• *No one is perfect.*
• *Every child is different.*
• *Just because you read a book, listened to a talk, podcast, or talked to your mentor, doesn't mean it will work with your child. (It's trial and error!) You, as the parent, must figure out exactly what works with your child and what doesn't work. You also need to take into consideration that what works during one stage of life will probably not work forever.*

Why is discipline important?

You've been entrusted with this child by God. Ask God to give you His full wisdom and knowledge.

COLOSSIANS 1:9
For this reason, since the day we heard about you, we have not stopped praying for you and asking God to fill you with the knowledge of his will through all spiritual wisdom and understanding.

Just talking about these things above, fear, anxiety, and other emotions are bubbling up in you. We've all been there; I've been there. Before you take notes, the best thing we can do today is to invite God into this conversation. And honestly, we have to do this every day with Him because you are going to walk away from today and feel empowered, but in a week you will be exhausted. So we need to get into the habit of going to God in prayer over discipline.

So, before we move forward, I want to pause and give us a moment to talk and rest with our Heavenly Father.

> *My prayer:*
> *God, remind these ladies, YOU chose these children for these specific moms.Whether adopted, fostering, or through natural birth, YOU chose them. Father, give us the wisdom to know what to do with these children. God, would you comfort these moms right now and show them they have not messed up? I pray Your mercy and grace over all of us today, that in YOU all things are made new, and Your mercies are new every morning.*

Moms, take a moment now and just talk to God. Open your heart and share your concerns and worries about discipline with Him.

Moms, I want to ask you to put your hands down on your lap and release your fear, anxiety, and insecurities to God. Release your child to Him. Now, I want you to flip your palms up and accept God's wisdom, knowledge, grace and mercy for you, as a mom.

Thank you for allowing me to pray over you.

Ladies, we can do this refocusing technique anytime throughout our day. Palms down/palms up, here is what I am releasing, here's what I'm receiving. Use this simple technique in your everyday life. It's an easy way to illustrate your dependence on God.

So, let's dive in.

Are you a morning or night person? I'm a morning person, and I love a wake-up call, but I don't like to be woken up by my children. I didn't like it when my children were young and they came in the middle of the night and said they threw up in their bed. I didn't like it when they would want to get in bed with me at 4 a.m.

I really didn't like it when I got a wake-up call concerning their behavior. You know, when you get the call or email from a teacher, from another mom, from someone in your neighborhood telling you that your child was involved in making unwise choices. What I mean by wake-up call is, when your child does something really alarming in their behavior and you are shocked as the mom, like, "Wow! When did this start happening?" That is a wake-up call.

I've found a child naturally pushs against the rules in four stages of life. These are the four stages of life where a child "wakes" up:

AGE	CHILD'S STAGE	PARENTS RESPONSE
2-4 YEARS OLD	Finding my voice	Shocked, makes excuses for child (i.e., tired, cutting teeth)
3RD-5TH GRADE	Testing my boundaries	Blame others
7TH-8TH GRADE	Fitting in	Parent fears that the child will go off the deep end
11TH-12TH GRADE	Becoming an adult	Clamp down or permissive

How should we respond?

2-4 YEARS:
Be ready for them to find their voice.

What does that look like?

- See your child as a sinner, not a saint. No one is perfect, not even your adorable princess or your handsome prince.
- Make a plan, not an excuse.
  (They're not tired or cutting molars; they are just being normal.)
- Be concise.
- Mean what you say and say what you mean.

As a mom, the worst thing you can do is throw out empty threats. If you are not going to follow through with what you are saying, then don't say it. Children are smart, and they will call your bluff.

- Be clear and do not reason.
  Whine: I can't understand you when you are talking that way.

- Be consistent.
  Schedules are important. Children learn through repetition.

- Remove emotions from your discipline.
  Children can be very manipulative, even at the young ages of 2-4 years old. They know how to get their way. Children learn how to charm the parent and make them so angry that the parent gives up. Children also learn how to pull on the heartstrings of a parent. For instance, your four-year-old might say, "It hurts me that you are mean to me." Or my favorite, "I don't like you when punish me."

AS PARENTS, WE MUST KEEP THE END PRODUCT IN MIND AND RISE ABOVE OUR CHILD'S SHIFTING EMOTIONS.
YOUR CHILD WILL NOT GET THERE ON HIS OWN.

3RD GRADE:
Don't overreact.

What does it look like for us not to overreact?

- Address the problem head on; do not run away.
  When Abby was in elementary school, she lied to her teacher about something. When she got in the car, she confessed it to me and I pulled the car over, listened to her, and forgave her. But I told her she needed to go confess to her teacher and ask for her forgiveness. Of course, Abby did not want to tell her teacher. She cried, but I made her do it. I knew that Abby needed to feel the full consequences of her actions to learn from her mistake. I knew it would be hard on Abby to walk back in the school and confess to her teacher. I also knew that her teacher would forgive Abby and welcome her with open arms (and she did). Abby learned a great lesson that day. *Our tendency is to change schools, friendships, blame others, but that is not always realistic.*

- Don't accept disrespect.
  No matter what age or phase your child is going through, disrespecting you (or other adults in positions of authority) is not acceptable. Call it out, explain why it is wrong, and take away privileges if necessary.

- Don't blame others.
  Children don't need to "learn" bad behavior. They all have a sinful nature; it is in all of us.

Moms, your children can handle reality; don't dumb it down for them because you are not doing them any favors in the long run.

7TH- 8TH GRADE:
Accept reality

What does it look like?

The pull of peer pressure is stronger than anything else in their lives. Remember when you were at this age? It is a fact that in middle school we ALL want to fit into the group. Middle school is an environment where hormones are high, and young people are trying to figure out who they are and where they belong. Therefore, it is a breeding ground for conformity. As a parent, you will be able to handle things better if you realize the factors that you are dealing with in your child.

Here's what you do:
- Get to know their friends.
- Be a neutral and safe advocate for your child.
- Be available and flexible—children open up at the oddest times, sometimes late at night or after you've spent some family time together.
- Don't expect the ride home from school to be the place where your child shares everything about the day.
- As a parent, the kiss of death is to tell (or imply to) your child you don't like their friend.
- Pick your battles because not everything is worth a fight.
- Remember that hormones are raging.
- Don't get drawn into the fight as children in middle school will fight about anything and everything. You become the enemy, and that justifies their behavior.
- Tell them there is nothing they can do to make you walk away from them.

16-18 YEARS OLD:
Be the coach

What does that look like?

- Give guidance.
- Discuss how consequences play out, whether good or bad.
- Meeting family expectations is not about rights; it's about privileges.
    - Car
    - Cell phone
    - After school activities

Obstacles to Discipline:

It takes a lot of work.
Stay-at-home moms are exhausted because they've been around the daily struggles of parenting all day. Don't give up moms! I know you are tired, but you got this!

Working moms want everyone to be happy. Working moms deal with people all day long, and they just want a few hours of joy. Working moms don't want to discipline when they get home, so a lot times they ignore the problem, either out of guilt or just being exhausted.

It is easy for all of us to be shortsighted. We think to ourselves, "This behavior will go away in a few years." But, moms, it won't; it will only get worse.

It's difficult to be on the same page as spouse.
Sometimes, your spouse will have a different perspective on discipline or on a specific situation than you. That's why it is so important to keep the lines of communication open and make sure that whatever the two of you decide is the best approach is supported by both parents. You should also talk to your spouse and ask him to support your decisions... and avoid situations where the two of you are playing "good cop/bad cop."

Reasons Why We Discipline

HEBREWS 12:11-12
No discipline seems pleasant at the time, but painful.
However, it produces a harvest of righteousness and peace for
those who have been trained by it.

Pain now equals
peace later

1. Harvest of righteousness and peace.
   Righteousness means excellence. We can all agree that we want our children to have a life of excellence and peace. To get to those two characteristics, we need to be disciplining our children.
2. Set the destination.
   Any great parent has a destination for their child, and the children are worth making the extra effort to get them there.

RESPONSIBLE
GIVING
LOVING

What is the destination for your child? **Where are you taking them?**

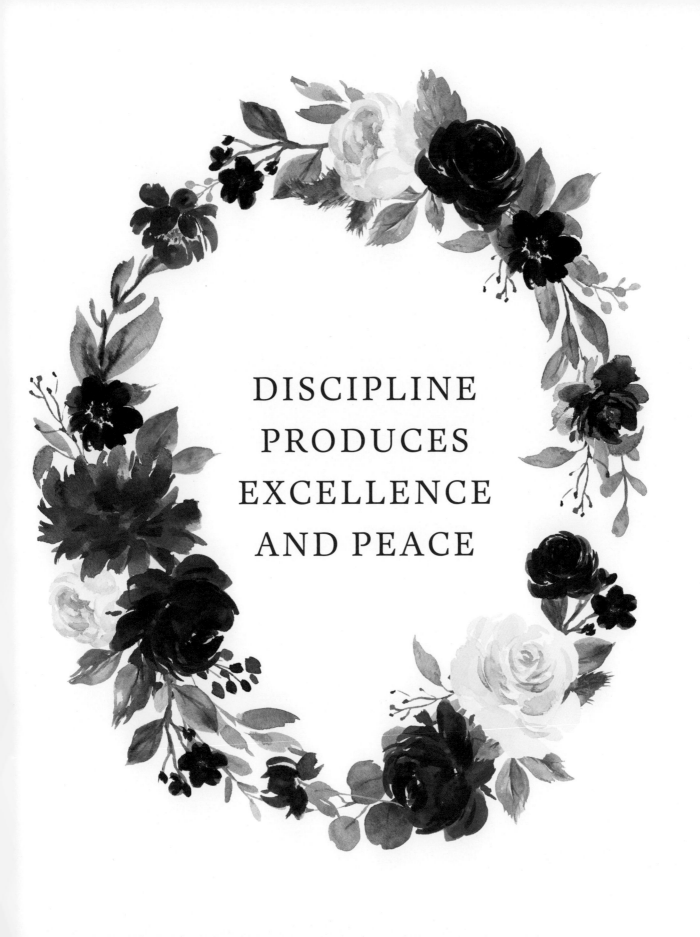

DISCIPLINE
PRODUCES
EXCELLENCE
AND PEACE

Moms, answer this question for yourself:

Why is discipline hard for you as a mom?

....

....

....

....

....

What can you change this week, either through your actions or in your mind, to help you?

....

....

....

....

....

....

....

....

REFLECT

As I think about the "hard" stages of motherhood, discipline was by far the hardest thing to do, but it changed the trajectory of my children. Teaching Kelsey to obey or submit to authority paid off in the long run. Teaching Emily why telling the truth was so important paid off.

Think about where you want your child to be in ten years. Make a plan now on how to get them there.

....

....

....

....

....

....

....

....

....

....

....

....

FINAL THOUGHT

We all want amazing children who will grow to be responsible and loving adults. In order for that to happen, we must train them up in the way they should go, and we do that through discipline. It may be unpleasant at times, but we love our children, and we need to do what is best for them. Keep in mind that parenting is a marathon, not a sprint. Disciplining your child takes time. Be patient.

Journal

....

....

....

....

....

....

....

....

....

A NOTE FROM KAREN

Moms,
I am praying for you in this journey to be strong and brave.
Lean into the Lord and not your own understanding. You've
got this! You are doing a great job!

Trust in the Lord u

lean not on your ow

your ways submit to

your pat

h all your heart and

nderstanding; in all

m, and He will make

straight.

PROVERBS 3:5-6 (NIV)

THE SCOREBOARD OF LIFE

W hen it comes to "life," we ALL have a scoreboard, don't we? Sure, my scoreboard may look different than yours, but because of our individual scoreboards, some of us may develop resentment over the slightest things. You may look at me and say, "Why are you so angry about that?" But, even though my life looks good to you, in my mind my scoreboard is I'm at 0, and my friend, husband, person on social media, woman at the gym, (fill in your person) they are at 10. They are winning.

In order for all of us to be on the same page, let's define what **resentmen**t is:

RESENTMENT IS THE FEELING OF ANGER OR DISPLEASURE ABOUT SOMEONE OR SOMETHING UNFAIR.

UNFAIR? I can name lots of things in life that I think are unfair, and I don't even have to think hard.

What are some examples of things that are unfair?

A husband's travel schedule, infertility, children with special needs, people who make more money than you, have nicer homes or cars than you, when your child doesn't get chosen for the travel ball team, when your daughter is not chosen for the recital, when you don't have a mom to call for support, when you can't find a job, when your husband loses his job unexpectedly, cancer, marital problems, being a single mom, health issues, when people seem to have it easier than you. We could keep going, but I think you get the point.

I fell into this way of thinking, of keeping score between Greg and myself, after our first child was born. After Kelsey arrived, I quit my job to be a stay-at-home mom, and Greg was selected for Top Gun in the Navy. Greg's life didn't change at all after we had Kelsey; his life seemed to get better. My life seemed to stop.

But, my life is not even that unfair in the whole scheme of things; it's just life. There are some moms who have it way harder than me, way more unfair than me.

Listen, you can go so far down this resentment road that you begin to regret your own life. You may want to trade your life and live another person's life.

Bottom line,
RESENTMENT IS BIG.

We all deal with resentment in different ways. Some of us get sarcastic *(you know what I'm talking about)*. We say, "Yeah, she's skinny, but nobody likes her." Or, "She exercises all the time, but I don't think she goes to church on Sunday, so if that is what I must do to look like that, I don't want it."

Some of us just get down on ourselves and throw ourselves a big ole pity party. And let's be honest, some of us, well, we just are mean about it.

The question for today is: *How do we handle a resentful spirit?*

PSALM 37:3-4
Trust in the Lord and do good;
dwell in the land and enjoy safe pasture.
Take delight in the Lord,
and he will give you the desires of your heart.

From these verses, we can find a formula. We all love a good formula, right?

Formula: Trust + Dwell + Cultivate = Rested Spirit

Trust in the Lord.
Dwell in the land, and rest in God.
Cultivate faithfulness...*Which means to do the **next** right thing.*

That is God's formula, but what we normally do (or what I normally do) is:

Trust ourselves + Anxiety+ Fear= Manipulation of forced outcomes

When I follow my formula, there is NO resting involved. I'm constantly thinking about my situation, how it is affecting me, how hard it is on me, or how it's not fair. I'm constantly talking about it, and I do not sit in faithfulness, doing the next right thing. I do quite the opposite. I do all the wrong things. I complain, whine, and manipulate. There's nothing right about any of that.

Some real-life examples?

I had a resentful spirit in those early years. In my mind, my life was HARD, and all my friends back home in Atlanta, they had it easy. Those friends didn't understand what sacrifice was or what defending your country looked like in the everyday world. No, those friends thought it was hard when their husbands had an overnight business trip. Please! One night away was a breeze! For me, it was weeks and weeks at a time.

Moms, I did not have a restful spirit; my spirit was tied up in knots, and I was very resentful and anxious about my future. Greg might not ever come back, for Heaven's sake!

Here's one that is super yucky! My house. Yes, you heard me right. For years (and I mean years), I was resentful over a house. I had a wonderful house, but I didn't like it. A great neighborhood with great people and a beautiful yard, but it wasn't what I wanted. It wasn't fair that I couldn't have the house I wanted. Other people had what I wanted. And talk about manipulation! Good grief, I was always talking about a new home, trying to think of ways we could afford it. Oh, I could go on and on. But, I will spare you the gory and ugly details because that is what resentment is — it is ugly!

Restful spirit? God's formula? What does that look like?

Let's go back to my time as a Navy wife. How did God bring me to a restful spirit? I learned to trust in Him. He had a plan for my life, and it wasn't in Georgia, but it was for me to find happiness in Virginia while Greg was in the Navy. I began to rest in God and stopped trying to write my story for Him, but allowed Him to write my story. I began to do the next right thing:

- To be kind and loving
- To be grateful
- To have a joyful heart

Ladies, trust is the foundation of a restful spirit.

TRUST IS WHAT CHANGES A RESENTFUL SPIRIT TO A RESTFUL SPIRIT.

To be the BEST version of a mom, a rested spirit is best. But, the question is HOW do we create a rested spirit? How do we build that kind of trust?

For me, it is easy to say, "Trust God," but in my resentful times, it was difficult to actually trust God because I felt like if I trusted Him, then I was giving up control. I didn't like that.

- When I trust God, I can't tell my sad story.
- If I give up control, I will lose control.

Trusting God is what changes a resentful spirit into a restful Spirit.

Trust isn't easy, but I have learned that God sees a different picture than me. **The whole formula depends on us trusting first and foremost.**

The reason we don't trust is because we don't see as God sees. If we could see how God sees, we would trust because then we would see the whole picture.

If you look at the back of a needlepoint, you will see knots, tie-offs, and a spot where a strand was cut. The back of the needlepoint is not pretty at all, but if you turn it over, there is a beautiful picture. Many times in our lives, we stay focused on the backside and do not see what God is creating and the beautiful artwork He alone is working on in our lives. We need to trust in God.

I know in my own life, I can look back and see where a knot led to freedom, where a tie-off wasn't something that was bad, but ended up being good. A cut was where I found brokenness, and in my brokenness is where I eventually found complete trust and peace in my life.

I am starting to see that what I used to make me feel resentful, God used in my story.

But, you may not be there yet. I have a lot of years on you. That is okay. God meets all of us where we are. He can handle where you are. He can handle the pain, and He knows the pain. Life may be a lot of things, but pain is involved if you live long enough. And when you are in the middle of the pain, "church-y" sayings don't help you.

I had a friend in Virginia who lost a child to SIDS. Her pain was real, and a simple religious statement didn't help her. At the baby's funeral, three people accepted Christ, and it's easy for you and me to see how God turned a very bad situation into something that was good. But, for my friend, there wasn't anything good about it. I remember we were talking one day, and she told me her mom said to her, "Isn't that good that three people came to know Christ because of the death of your child?" My friend looked at her mom and said, "I don't care how many people came to Christ. My son is dead. I'm angry."

That is real life. But, God is okay with real life. If you are wrestling with resentment, that is okay. I want this to be a safe place for you. You have the freedom to wrestle, to cry out, to scream, 'That's not fair!' God is okay with that.

Even Jesus wrestled with His faith. But, you cannot STAY in the wrestling; you eventually need to make a choice.

For some of us today, we are hiding in wrestling versus choosing to trust.

For others of us today, we need to start connecting to the fact that God is showing you a picture. It may not be the picture you had in mind, or one that you want, but it is the picture He is giving you.

There are some of us who are choosing to remain resentful forever, and I want to encourage you to let that go.

There are only two choices:
- Hold onto resentment.
- Rest in the fact that God can be trusted.

Apostle Peter showed us this choice when he was struggling with how things were going for him.

We read in John 6:68 that this was a big shift for Peter, and he said it best, "To whom shall I go?"

My friend in Virginia who lost her child eventually gave up her resentment, cried out to God, and He met her where she was. She had been a Christian since she was a little girl, so when she thought, "To whom shall I go?" God was her choice.

RESPOND

What are the areas in your life where you are keeping score?

....

....

....

What is holding you back from trusting in God?

....

....

....

....

....

....

....

....

....

....

....

How long have you had a resentful spirit?

....

....

....

....

If you were to trust God today, what would that look like for you?

....

....

....

....

....

....

....

....

....

....

....

FINAL THOUGHT

In your time alone today, I would love for you to pause, think about and answer these two questions:

- Are you running toward resentment?
- Are you trusting God to help you meet resentment head-on?

What do you do when the scoreboard of life is showing you are down and everyone else is up? That your kids are average, your husband doesn't love you the way your friend's husband loves her, you have it hard in life, or more? You and I have a choice when the scoreboard doesn't seem fair, and our choice will determine whether our spirit remains resentful or rested.

I don't know about you, but I don't want to live a resentful life or have the fruit of a resentful life: sarcasm, bitterness, no joy.

I can't stay resentful and trust God at the same time.

One thing is defining your relationship with God and probably with other people.

But the reason we don't trust is because we don't see as God sees. Join me today and ask God to open your eyes and show you a bigger picture for your life.

Journal

....

....

....

....

....

....

....

A NOTE FROM KAREN

Moms,
Hanging onto resentment only hurts you. I became a much happier person when I stopped keeping score with people. My prayer for you is that you will choose joy today to rest in God.

Trust in the Lord a[nd]
dwell in the land a[nd]
Take delight in the [Lord]
and he will give yo[u]
heart. PSALM 37: 3-4

d do good;
 enjoy safe pasture.
ord,
 he desires of your

Session Six
FINDING YOU AGAIN

I have a podcast, Wire Talk with Karen Stubbs, and on this podcast, moms write in the questions they have concerning motherhood. I began to get more questions like the ones below, which led me to realize these moms' questions represented a lot of moms' questions.

How can I be a great mom without losing who I am?
How can I distinguish who I am from what I do?

I know I have wrestled with these questions. I think most moms tend to lose themselves in motherhood. There are a few big obstacles that stand in the way of us finding ourselves as women.

Three of the biggest obstacles are:

1. Everyone else comes before mom.
From the moment we bring our newborns home from the hospital, we put the baby's needs before our own, which is a good thing. As the baby grows, however, we continue to put their needs before our own, until one day, we stop realizing that we have needs. In that process, we lose a part of ourselves.

2. The world of motherhood can be lonely.
Being a mom can be very isolating. No one prepares a mom for that reality. A mom's world usually revolves around a child's schedule, and because of that, she is home most of the time by herself, which can lead to feelings of being away from the action and loneliness.

3. The pendulum of motherhood swings from one extreme to another. There is always tension between two sides of motherhood. On one side, there is the irresponsible mom who is not involved in her child's life. *(You are not this mom, because if you were, you wouldn't be doing a study on motherhood.)*

On the other side, there is the martyr mom to whom family is everything. This mom can be a stay-at-home mom, or a working mom who can't do anything for herself when she gets home because she feels guilty about working. In either case, this mom doesn't have a life of her own, only the life of her family, which becomes her life. When her children leave the home as adults, she is lost, has no purpose, and gets very depressed.

WE ALL NEED TO TAKE STEPS TO BECOMING THE MOM IN THE MIDDLE. WE GET TO THE MIDDLE OF THE PENDULUM BY PRACTICING SELF-CARE.

Examples of self-care:
- Be the mom who can say "no" to her children. These can be small no's like, "You may not have a bite of my ice cream; you had yours, and this is mine." Or they may be larger no's like, "I cannot go to all 50 of your baseball games. I will be on my annual trip with your dad on one of those games."
- Be the mom that splurges every so often on something for herself: clothes, yard, house, mani-pedi.
- Be the mom that invests time in pursuing interests that are important to her, whether a hobby, volunteer work, writing, or starting a business.
- Be the mom who takes time to exercise to clear her head and take care of herself.

When I think of self-care, I think of this verse:

ISAIAH 30:15
This is what the Sovereign Lord, the Holy One of Israel says,
"In repentance and rest is your salvation."

Definition of salvation: deliverance from harm, ruin or loss.

If you want to be saved as a mom, this verse is pure gold.
We all want the end product of a great healthy family, but...

WE CAN'T EXPORT A HEALTHY FAMILY IF WE CAN'T EXPORT A HEALTHY US.

Two things are required to export a healthy us:

Rest & Repentance

Rest
Rest is not just a thing to do, but in Scripture, is a requirement:

Examples:
- **God rested on the seventh day.**
    - Genesis 2:2-3: *By the seventh day God had finished the work he had been doing; so on the seventh day he rested from all his work. Then God blessed the seventh day and made it holy, because on it he rested from all the work of creating that he had done.*

- **Psalm 23**

- **Jesus models this as He retreats.**
    - Matthew 14:23: *After he had dismissed them, he went up on a mountainside by himself to pray.*

As moms, we are doing an important thing, but Jesus's mission was to save the world! And yet, he took time to get away, to rest and pray.

What does it look like to rest?

Definition: To cease work or movement in order to relax, refresh oneself, or recover strength.

5 Ways To Know When You Need Rest

- Are you forgetful?
- Are you exhausted?
- Are you anxious?
- Do you manage your family's schedule, or does their schedule manage you? For example, do you set nap time, bedtime, playtime, and rest time? Or does it just happen?
- Do you find that your down time is filled with errands, watching TV, or technology? If yes, then you are not resting. Your brain is still working.

Moms, you don't have a choice; your body needs rest. You can either give it the rest that it needs, or it will begin to shut down through anxiety, depression, aches and pains, or complete exhaustion.

Here are some examples of how I have chosen to rest at different times:

- Vacationing in Key West with Greg
- Visiting a friend in Washington, DC, or a friend in Boston
- Taking a long bath
- Treating myself to a manicure

Some of you may need a vacation away from home, either by yourself or with your husband. Others may be able to find a little sanctuary closer to home:

- spa
- hotel
- movie in the afternoon
- a night out to just talk, vent, or laugh with a friend

Give yourself time to know what your need is.

When you begin to prioritize yourself, be prepared because false guilt will more than likely set in. Resist that! You are going to be a BETTER mom because of the rest.

Remind yourself that God Himself prioritized rest, and He doesn't see you as being lazy or selfish.

Repentance

What is it that keeps you from resting? Is it a case of the "what ifs?"

What if:
- The kids won't be taken care of? Nobody can take care of them like me.
- The girls won't eat well? The babysitter doesn't watch what they eat.
- My boys will miss me? I don't want my child to cry or be sad.

This is a need for CONTROL.

Confess that need to God, and learn to let it go.

Maybe some of you need to repent for thinking of yourself as unworthy, for not measuring up. You may think that you don't deserve to rest. You may need to take some time and confess to God that you have insulted His child, His creation, His pride and joy... you. You need to ask God to forgive you for not loving yourself, not loving what He created.

You don't want to be the mom who experiences a loss of yourself.
You don't want to be the mom who is harmed by not knowing who you are.
You don't want to be the mom who is lost when her child graduates.

RESPOND

Being a mom is draining. What areas do you see where you need to refuel?

....

....

....

....

....

....

....

....

....

....

....

....

....

....

Recognizing your need to refuel is the first step. The second step is taking action. What can you do this week to pour into yourself?

....

....

....

What can you implement over the next year?

....

....

....

Where do you want to be in ten years?

....

....

....

....

....

....

....

FINAL THOUGHT

Ask yourself these two questions and be honest:

What do you need to confess?
Where do you need to find rest?

When you choose rest, it gives your body, mind, and spirit time to recharge. In that recharging, you will start to discover things about yourself that you forgot, or learn new things about yourself.

Rest is the first step toward finding you again—or better yet, discovering the new and improved you!

I promise you, if you do these two things, you WILL find you again. God created you, you are HIS idea, and He knows how to save you from everything—including yourself. And He has plans for you.

Journal

....

....

....

....

....

....

....

....

"WE CAN'T EXP
FAMILY IF WE
HEALT

RT A HEALTHY

AN'T EXPORT A

Y US."

KAREN STUBBS

A NOTE FROM KAREN

Moms,
You are beautiful, created by God. Being a mom is only part
of who you are — don't lose yourself in motherhood. Let your
children see the whole person and all your giftings.
